WHERE DO BIRDS LIVE?

Ron Hirschi

photographs by
Galen Burrell

Walker and Company
New York

For Ken Short

First published in the United States of America in 1987 by the
Walker Publishing Company, Inc.

Library of Congress Cataloging-in-Publication Data

Hirschi, Ron.
  Where do birds live?

  Summary: Examines where birds live, looking at such
natural habitats as ponds, rivers, old trees, mountains,
and backyards.
  1. Birds—Habitat—Juvenile literature. [1. Birds—
Habitat] I. Burrell, Galen, ill. II. Title.
QL676.2.H57 1987   598.2'52   87-16063
ISBN 0-8027-6722-2
ISBN 0-8027-6723-0 (lib. bdg.)

Printed in Hong Kong

10 9 8 7 6 5 4 3 2 1

Book design by Laurie McBarnette

WHERE DO BIRDS LIVE?

Birds live in quiet places.

They live where they can
watch the morning come.

Birds live in spring
blossoms,

cold winter snow

and prickly cactus in
summer heat.

Birds live alone.

Some live with others.

Some live with so many you
could not count them all.

Birds live in shrubby tangles,
in houses you make for them,

in lakes and streams where
they can take a bath

and in trees older than
anyone can remember.

Some live far away in the
wilderness—

but many birds live in your
own backyard.

AFTERWORD

Birds live in all these places and many more. This introduction to the special places where birds live offers young readers a chance to think about where they see birds. We hope it also helps them understand that each bird has its own needs—and that many kinds of places are needed so that the world might always be filled with the beauty of birds.

Note on the habitat of each bird

Cover: Pine Grosbeaks live in the northern woodlands of North America, Europe, and Asia as well as in the American West.

Back cover: Common Goldeneye

Frontispiece: Western Tanagers brighten mornings in the West, especially in mountain forests.

Quiet Places (inset): Trumpeter Swans nest along rivers and lakes in the Rocky Mountains, where they are still rare after being very near extinction.

Quiet Places (background): Mountain Bluebirds nest in tree cavities in mountainous areas of the West, ranging from Alaska to the mountains of Mexico.

Morning come (inset): Western Tanager

Morning come (background): Trumpeter Swan

Spring blossoms (inset): Pine Siskins are friendly birds usually seen in flocks high in the trees. They enjoy sunflower seeds.

Spring blossoms (background): Cedar Waxwings prefer fruits and berries, usually traveling in flocks to search for their favorite trees.

Winter snow (inset): Dark-eyed Juncos are also known as snowbirds. They are often seen at backyard feeders, but they nest on the ground in the forest.

Winter snow (background): Northern Pintails are elegant ducks that can usually be seen at the shallow edges of fresh or saltwater marshes, where they feed on tiny shrimp, insects, and seeds.

Cactus (inset): Curve-billed Thrashers live in the desert Southwest where they often tuck their nests of thorny twigs into the prickly branches of a cholla cactus.

Cactus (background): Organ Pipe National Monument, Arizona.

Alone (inset): Bald Eagles soar over open water in search of fish, ducks, and other prey. They need huge old trees for their stick nests since the nest is added to each year and may grow to be 12 feet deep and 8 feet across.

Alone (background): Barred Owls live in forests of the East and North as well as in southern swamps. Like many owls, they nest in tree cavities.

With others (inset): White Pelicans always seem to enjoy the company of other pelicans as they drift on rivers or lakes, scooping up fish.

With others (background): Sandhill Cranes may nest in fairly small marshes or along the banks of streams, but they prefer large, open fields and prairie during much of the year. As they soar across the western sky, they seem to own the prairie wind.

So many others (inset): Canada Geese live together in family flocks throughout North America and parts of Europe. They know one another well.

So many others (background): Bohemian Waxwings travel in large flocks, usually nesting in the northern coniferous forests of northwestern North America as well as the northern regions of Europe and Asia.

Houses (inset): The House Wren is the common wren of the East and the small bird you might expect to move in if you put up a birdhouse in your own backyard.

Shrubby tangle (background): Dark-eyed Junco in red osier dogwood.

Lakes and streams (inset): American Wigeons often feed in grassy fields and golf courses. Their soft whistle can also be heard along the East and West coasts, especially in salt marshes.

Lakes and streams (background): Dippers dive beneath the surface of fast-flowing western streams, plunging into the water in search of small fish and aquatic insects. They swim with wings outstretched and cling to mossy river rocks with their strong toes.

Old trees (inset): Yellow-rumped warblers snatch insects from branches of trees. They are one of the most abundant warblers of North America.

Old Trees (background): Young Bald Eagle perched in old tree along a western river.

Wilderness (inset): Roseate Spoonbills live in the shallows and marshes of the Gulf of Mexico and Florida Bay. They catch fish and shrimp with their unique bill and attract our attention with their beautiful feathers.

Wilderness (background): Barn Swallows are very widespread, building their mud nests on houses and barns throughout North America. I wonder where they built their nests before there were barns?

Your Backyard (inset): Bohemian Waxwings on fence.

Your Backyard (background): Yellow-headed Blackbirds nest in marshes, but they can be seen in many places during migration.

NOTE ON MIGRATORY HABITS OF BIRDS

Like the Yellow-headed Blackbird, many birds fly to new surroundings after the nesting season. Many warblers migrate from the northern edges of North America to Mexico or Central and South America for the winter. For some birds, migration is a time to fly to lower elevations to avoid cold, winter snow, and ice. Mountain Bluebirds will leave the high country in winter, and the Dippers will too, especially when their streams begin to freeze over.

Bird migration remains a wonderful mystery in many ways. We do know that birds seem able to return to their favorite nesting places year after year. Some birds also fly thousands of miles along migratory routes, being guided by familiar sights, sounds, and clues we are not aware of unless we begin to think like birds. However, many birds do not migrate and some individuals of a migratory species decide for reasons of their own, not to migrate. Why? Maybe you will be the special person to discover that answer.